ON AN AMATEUR MOM

★ The image of 'Mom' was drawn by our daughter, Janette, at age 7.

Renee Thomas Hawkley

Once Upon an Amateur Mom
Copyright © 2023 by Renee Thomas Hawkley

RHG Media Productions
25495 Southwick Drive #103
Hayward, CA 94544.

ISBN 979-8-9890542-0-6 (paperback)
ISBN 979-8-9890542-1-3 (hardcover)

Visit us on line at www.YourPurposeDrivenPractice.com
Printed in the United States of America.

WHAT PEOPLE ARE SAYING

"'Once Upon an Amateur Mom' is a fabulous tribute to real-life motherhood."
—**Blair Wood,** investor

"This collection of Renee's experiences as a mom speaks the language of moms everywhere."
—**Carolyn Tanner Reese,** seasoned elementary school teacher

"A delightful read that is real, tender, and cleverly written!"
—**Denise Wyatt,** homemaker, care giver, and grandma of ten

"What fun tidbits on mothering to bring a smile to my face. I enjoy the wit, the humor, the perspective, and the wisdom Renee shares."
—**Karla Briggs,** former elementary ed teacher

"Heartfelt and honest musings and antidotes on the joy, and sometimes not so joyous occasions of being a mom. I loved every page."
—**Kris Ellis**, former Idaho legislator and currently a property manager

"With wit and a lively sense of humor, Renee captures the precious moments when 'young parents' wonder if they are actually 'doing any good' in their early days of parenting."
—**Dr. Vincent Muli Wa Kituku**, motivational speaker, author, and creator of Kenya's www.caringheartsandhandsofhope.org

"A family love story . . . past, present and future . . . Renee's family and faith have brought joy, strength and peace."
-Delma Atwell, mother of six, grandmother of eleven

DEDICATION

With appreciation to my friends,
Barbara Morrill and Robyn Nguyen,
who asked me to share.

Mom . . .

*A word is worth
a thousand pictures.*

SECTIONS

SECTION 1

BEING A MOM

'Mother' Is a Verb

It's like this. Mothers are mothers because they *do* what they *do,* and what they *do* best is nurture life.

I met a dear friend on the pages of a book who makes this point clearly and void of pride. She nurtured millions with little words and little deeds of love that translated into big differences around the world. Is there a mother more deserving of the title than the saintly Mother Teresa, who never gave birth to a single person? Not in my book.

The memory of Mother Teresa's service, offered to young and old, healthy and maimed, rich and poor, saint or sinner is clearly documented and now, legendary.

My friend, Helen, a teacher by profession, married a widower and helped him raise his children. She and her husband created an agency that connects needy children from many nations to adoptive parents. She is thus a mother and grandmother of many families, including their own.

Lalinda, my email friend, has physical limitations that have prevented her from marrying. She '*mothers*' cats with tender devotion.

Another friend, Ruth, nurtures wounded birds back to health and rejoices as they take to the skies once again and fly away.

Sandi cares for Raylene's school-age children by attending their activities and games while Raylene works night and day as a single mother of six children to reach her goal of earning a doctoral degree.

Another mother fosters eight special needs children until she is able to legally adopt them. The stories of a mother's love are unending.

Why do mothers **do** these things?

If you're a woman who nurtures life, I suspect that you have a few answers to that question since, by title and by talent, you are a mother.

You're a Mom When . . .

Y ou know you're a mom when:

- you never leave home without soda crackers and *'Fruit Snacks.'*
- you replace eye makeup with handy-wipes in your purse.
- you give the nurse the *'evil eye'* when he gives your child a shot.
- you label yourself as *The Big Apple . . . 'the city that never sleeps.'*
- you cut your husband's pancakes with a pizza cutter.
- your closest friend is *Sam I Am.*
- you accept a nine-month pregnancy as the intro class in Patience.
- you can see what happens behind you without turning your head.
- you purchase bathroom accessories only if they match grape jelly.
- you lick your thumb and wipe cherry juice off your own face.
- you think of a trip alone to the grocery store as a night out.
- you start wearing white ankle socks.
- you can identify the brand of peanut butter in one bite.
- you stop seeing fingerprints on walls and windows.
- you consider Dr. Seuss as your analyst.
- you look forward to hugs and butterfly kisses more than a massage.
- you offer your father a dish of ice cream after he eats his broccoli.

- you can feed the baby and talk on the phone at the same time.
- you get evicted from Little League games for yelling at referees.
- you think of the bathroom as a sanctuary.
- you sing '*I'm a little teapot*' in the shower.

Keeping My Mouth Shut

I'm almost never sorry when I keep my mouth shut.

I've been sorry for opening it, though.

Like the times I said:

- *'Morning sickness is an old wive's tale.'*
- *'Pregnant women who waddle look ridiculous.'*
- *'Labor and delivery is a natural process. How bad could it be?'*
- *'Breast-fed babies don't get colic.'*
- *'The book says potty training takes a couple of weeks.'*
- *'Be sure to call if you have trouble with the kids while we're gone.'*
- *'I refuse to pay for inferior quality. That's why I learned to sew.'*
- *'Peanut butter and jelly sandwiches are a cop-out.'*
- *'Sure. I'll be room mother again.'*
- *'Having a clean house is just a matter of priorities.'*
- *'Why do you suppose she talks so much in class?'*
- *'Where did you come up with an idea like that?'*
- *'When was the last time I raised my voice at you?'*
- *'Pile in. The more the merrier!'*
- *'I can't believe they let their kids do that.'*
- *'The secret is to keep track of your teenagers.'*
- *'You're grounded for a month.'*
- *'Give me three good reasons why I should say yes.'*
- *'I said good reasons.'*
- *'I said GOOD reasons.'*

- *'If you have questions about sex, come ask me.'*
- *'I know more about sex than your teacher.'*

And . . . the absolute best way to lose an audience or a friend:
'I just have one more story to tell you about my grandchildren.'

Mothers Worry Best

In the *Triple Crown of Worry*, mothers are first out of the gate and last to cross the finish line because there's a lot to worry about. For example:

We worry about what our children *CAN* do. For instance, they learn new skills like kayaking, rock climbing and mountain biking, then proceed to uncharted locations with their buddies to practice their new skills.

We worry about what our children *CAN'T* do. They can't sit still in church. They can't swallow a pill or keep their shoes tied. They can't go to sleep.

We worry about what they *WILL* do. They will take a Band-aid off as soon as it is covering the scratch. They will scrape their knees, pick their noses and belch in public.

We worry about what they *WON'T* do. They won't go to bed. They won't pay attention to directions or logic. They won't *'go potty'* on demand.

We worry about what they *SHOULD* do. They should eat their vegetables, drink their milk and help with the dishes. They should remember to take a jacket to a November football game.

We worry about what they *SHOULDN'T* do. They shouldn't try a first cigarette just for the fun of seeing if they like it. They shouldn't cross the street before looking both ways.

We worry about what they *MIGHT* do. They might break curfew. They might lose their retainers. They might tip over when the training wheels come off their bikes.

We worry about what they might *NOT* do. They might not fasten their seat belts when *'cruising'* with friends. They might not stop picking scabs.

We worry about what they *DO*. They run when they should walk. They walk when they should run. They forget to complete the homework they hid under their bed, but remember the last time you yelled at them in great detail.

We worry about what they *DON'T* do. They don't clean their rooms. They don't come home on time. They don't brush their teeth before bed without being reminded, and they seldom floss.

Over the years, mothers turn worry into an art form. The reason I'm sure of this is, when leaving my Mom's house after visiting my parents when they were in their 80s, Mom would set her alarm clock and call me when three-and-a-half hours had passed just to make sure I had arrived home safely.

Just between you and me, I think Mom still worries about me, even though she no longer operates on this planet . . . and I like that.

* 'My mother, Verla Price Thomas (1914-2008), continues to be my North Star.'

No Comfort Zone For Moms

I t's hard for moms to get into a *'comfort zone'* because there are always *'new and improved ways and means'* for moms to goof up. Here's a modest sample from my bucket of memories:

- Driving into the side of a hospital after an appointment with my obstetrician, who had just delivered the news that I might be carrying twins.
- Starting to mix a batch of bread dough in the largest container I had at the time, which was an 8-cup mixing bowl.
- Taking my eyes off our three-year-old son as he was pushing a stroller in a crowd of 100,000 at a Fourth of July fireworks celebration in Washington, DC.
- Forgetting to tell a van load of teenagers when and where to meet after dropping them off at the Twin Falls Mall.
- Driving ten miles in the direction of home before discovering I had left our five-year-old son at church.
- Putting a gallon container of honey on the bottom shelf of the cupboard.
- Telling our son he did *Not* have to go to the bathroom right this very minute.

It's reassuring to know that other moms have similar and even *'better'* stories. For example, my sister-in-law, Karen, copied a favorite lasagna recipe for her newlywed daughter, but made the mistake of writing ¼ *'cup'* pepper instead of ¼ *'teaspoon.'* The happy couple reported that the lasagna they baked was *'pretty spicy.'*

The benefits of *'family goof-ups'* add up over the years, as memories are repeated again and again, and nobody says, *'You're fired!'*

Three Little Words

Mothers are masters of *'cut to the chase'* conversations.

Here's a sample of their *'three-little-words'* directives:

Brush your teeth.
Comb your hair.
Come and eat.
Make your bed.
Wash your face.
Tie your shoes.
Pick it up.
Find your coat.
Listen to me!
Just a minute.
Wipe your nose.
Put it away.
Flush the toilet!
Clean your room.
Oh, I guess.
Hang it up.
Shut the door.
Who did that?
Don't lose it.
I said *'no.'*
Turn it down!
Tell Mommy, *'Potty.'*
Get a haircut.

Break it up!
Empty the garbage.
Wash your hands.
Call your sister.
Turn it off.
Not so fast!
Where's the aspirin?
Leave her alone.
Let Mommy sleep.
Bring that home.
Open the door.
Yes, you can.
Turn it off.
Stop teasing her!
No more fighting.
Do your homework.
No more cookies.
Come straight home.
No means no.
You did what?
Go to bed.
Say your prayers.
What's that noise?
No more drinks.
No more popcorn.

There are good reasons why mothers keep at it day after day, month after month and year after year. Three little words . . . I love you!

The Trouble with Mother

The trouble with Mother is;

She has too many rules.
She makes me eat green stuff.
She scrubs behind my ears.
She buys shoes instead of toys.
She tells me to burp on the inside.
She takes me to the dentist.
She keeps reminding me to flush.
She hides candy and cookies.
She washes my face without asking.
She brushes my teeth again if I only missed one.
She says '*clean*' too much.
She asks questions.
She says '*Go to bed*' before I want to.
She rubs sunscreen on me all over.
She buys milk instead of root beer.
She turns the TV off in the middle of the show.
She tells me what I'm thinking.
She talks too much.
She buys boring cereal.
She takes my temperature.
She looks under my bed.
She thinks soap is smoother than dirt.
She wakes me up before I'm ready.
The trouble with Mother is — she's good for me!

A Mother's Creed

I am a mother.
I link humanity's past to its future.
My moment in history is today.
As a precious pearl in the strand of time,
I add love and light and luster to the timeless
Thread of life that fastens me to generations past.
My task is both common and noble.
I share it with peasants and queens.
I will not belittle my part,
For I have a title role in the play of life.
My little words and deeds, though small, will one day
eclipse those of governments and kingdoms.
My achievement will endure when even time is a memory;
For I am a mother . . .
I link humanity's past to its future.

SECTION 2

CHILDREN

A Child is a Wonderful Thing

I carry the title of 'grown up,' but I like children better.

Children are . . . well . . . children. They work hard at goofing around. They sit at the edge of puddles and squeeze black, oozy mud between their toes. They say they're six-and-a-half-going-on-seven because they can hardly wait for more life to arrive. They dash toward time with an eager embrace and a slobbery kiss instead of trying to squirm free of it.

Children find joy in simple things, like the tickle of a yellow dandelion on their necks, a grape popsicle, the silky softness of a rabbit's fur, or the sight of an angleworm on a rainy sidewalk.

Children welcome challenges. Who can peel the largest patch of skin from sunburned bodies? Who can build a sandcastle to defy the tide? Who can skip a rock three times on the surface of a lake? Who can hide in a pile of leaves? Who can count the stars?

Children take the guesswork out of human relations. They're not stingy with their feelings. When you smile at them, they smile back. When they're sad or hurt or afraid, they cry on the outside. When somebody takes their favorite toy, they don't analyze it or consider all the angles. They just get it back.

Children don't know about 'can't.' They can and will try anything. In spite of bumps, bruises, scrapes and broken bones, they keep getting back up and trying again until they've mastered walking, riding a bike, rollerskating, soccer and whatever challenges they choose to figure out.

Children are believers. They make wishes before they blow out the candles. They throw pennies into fountains and cast their favorite dreams at the first star to appear in the vast night sky. They search for four-leaf clovers until they find one because they believe in luck, and they sing *'Lady bug, lady bug, fly away home'* as if the lady-bugs are listening. They think they won't get a sunburn.

Children are forgiving. They can't be bothered with nursing grudges. One moment, they dub you as *'the meanest mother in the world,'* and five minutes later, they stamp your cheek with a slobbery kiss after eating a twist of licorice.

Children bend. They haven't made plans. They aren't square-fillers, watch wearers, calendar-keepers or card-carriers. The only moment they're invested in is this one.

Children are creative. They never walk if they can skip, hop, jump or run. They never talk if they can giggle, chatter or squeal. They never look if they can inspect or peek. They never smell if they can sniff. They live life with *'gusto.'*

Children are optimists. They think they can walk to Grandma's house. They think they can save their allowance and buy a Corvette.

Children are understanding. They don't carry around a written or unwritten list of standards for other people's lives.

Children are curious. They have a million questions, like *'Where does God live?'* or *'Do water skippers have muscles?'* They think every question has an answer.

Children are trusting. They're ready to deliver two or three hugs for every one they receive. A hug fixes anything. They understand the most important rules in life are short: *'Love me,'* and *'Be nice.'*

Children are as fresh as unsliced bread. They're the treasure no money can buy. They're unpredictable, underrated and unappreciated until they're marching in step with the *'grown-ups.'* Children are full of wonder and wonderful.

It's puzzling. We devote our childhoods to doing what comes naturally, in love with the magic and mastery of life in all its wondrous simplicity. As grown-ups, we spend the rest of our lives working to recapture it.

Children are the best way to start people.

Children Provide Brain Munchies

Providing brain munchies for adults is one of the things children do best. For example, at a local elementary school, a bulletin board displayed one classroom's punch lines for common sayings that are unfamiliar to children.

Here are a few:

The pen is mightier than . . . the eraser.

It's always darkest before . . . bedtime.

In every cloud, there's a . . . bunch of raindrops.

You can lead a horse to water, but . . . don't get behind it.

Laugh and the world laughs with you. Cry and . . . you get a runny nose.

Happy the bride that . . . gets the cake.

Never underestimate the power of . . . school.

Don't bite the hand that . . . belongs to your mom.

Money is the root of . . . buying.

If you lie down with the dogs . . . they will probably get up and run away.

A penny saved is . . . not a lot.

Children are to be seen and not . . . hurt.

A bird in the hand is worth . . . buying a cage.

The grass is always greener on the other side of . . . a fire hydrant.

And, my personal favorite:

There's no business like . . . McDonald's.

The Climb

My little one plops his tiny form sideways
at the crown of the hill
and tumbles gleefully down
Over and over and head over heels
until his joy
is swallowed by the level place
With never a thought of the effort
as he bounds up
to retrace the ascent and regain the top
Again and again in
a singular oneness with the universe.
Ah, sweet, brief childhood!
How much longer will he savor
the treasure of his new home
before channeling the strain and drudgery
of the climb?

SECTION 3
FAITH

The Necklace

It was painful to pull the small silver cocoon tangled in towel lint out of the dryer and discover it contained the earthly remains of a treasured necklace. Our daughter, Jill, had given it to me as a gift. It displayed her birthstone and the birthstones of her siblings. Now, it was ruined due to my careless mistake.

I placed the little wad of guilt into a small dish on my dresser, promising to attempt a recovery later . . . when I had time. Later became a year, maybe two. In the meantime, I felt pangs of regret often as I glanced at the little tangle of matted silver mixed with threads from a towel.

One day, I decided I had suffered long enough. It was time to see if even a small part of the necklace could be salvaged. I gathered tools . . . a magnifying glass, a piece of black velvet to serve as a *'jeweler's background,'* a pair of needle-nosed tweezers . . . and went to work.

I was encouraged when the tight grip of the tangles loosened ever so slightly to my gentle urgings. I was disappointed to discover that several of the stones were missing and then elated to find both ends of the necklace with clasp and clasp receiver intact! A few more overs, under, around and throughs, and the truth lay before me.

The delicate chain was free and unbroken! The process had taken less than an hour instead of the three I had budgeted. Luckily, the replacement stones were still being sold and were easily replaced.

I hope to wear my beautiful necklace for many years to come, but there's more. I learned something. Next time I get stuck in guilt after making one of those big or small mistakes that are common to my species, I'm not going to punish myself for so long before deciding on a plan to take tiny steps in the direction of *'fixing and forgiving.'*

Because, as it turns out, those tiny steps forward toward reconciliation will lead to an entry door that closes behind me and stops the endless *'should-a,' 'would-a,'* and *'could-a'* reminders that feed pointless, guilt-ridden yearnings to go back in time and change the unchangeable.

There is the Joy

There is the joy
of feeling the trust of a child as her tiny
hand nestles gently in mine.
There is the joy
of receiving a heart emoji from the son
who asked me to leave them out.
There is the joy
of helping a neighbor rake leaves on a brisk autumn day.
There is the joy
of singing next to the best soprano in the
choir, pretending her voice is my own.
and
There is the joy
of Jesus knowing my name, my hopes, and my sorrows.
There is the joy
of offering my trust, my heart and hands to Him.
and
There is the joy
of letting go of everything else.
" . . . his hand is stretched out still."
Isaiah 9:12, 17, 21

A Lesson On Folding Laundry

I enjoy folding laundry, and I'm good at it. After watching a laundry-folding demonstration on TV that featured a famous celebrity and a long counter, I gave myself an A+. My family of ten has provided me with the opportunity to perfect the talent of folding any article that comes out of the dryer without a long counter and in mid-air. What can I say?

Sometimes while I'm folding laundry, I think about the complex creations that make up our world. In the dryer, each unique piece of laundry tumbles in an atmosphere of warmth, freedom and spontaneity.

In all my years of folding laundry, I've never opened the dryer at the end of a cycle to discover a single sock, dishrag, t-shirt or pair of pants that had folded itself into a pattern of order without my expertise.

I get it. Folding laundry isn't a talent that deserves much notice in comparison to the creation of Niagara Falls, an orchid or even an ant. Every day, the sun appears in the east at a specified moment as noted by weather experts. Planets follow their designated processes, and life on earth continues its course. Rivers find their way to oceans, oceans do their part in weather patterns, and seasons change. Life comes and goes.

And I wonder. How long would the atoms in all these systems have to tumble through eons of space and time before managing to arrange themselves into predictable, orderly processes? Reason and experience teach me it would take a lot longer than the time it would take for a batch of laundry to fold itself into neat stacks at the end of a dryer cycle.

There is a God.

We can't begin to appreciate or acknowledge the intelligence and love demonstrated in the magnificence of His creations. I think about that sometimes as I'm folding a batch of laundry and placing the organized stacks into their specific drawers and closets for my family.

Top Ten Things Jesus Never Said

10. Get lost.
9. What's in it for me?
8. That would take a miracle.
7. Take a number.
6. Who cares?
5. I'll need your photo ID.
4. Your account is overdrawn.
3. This call will be recorded.
2. Who do you think you are?
1. You got yourself into this mess, and you can get yourself out.

Mothers Harmonize To Make A Difference

I grew up in the sheltered community of Shelley, Idaho. One childhood memory is *The Singing Mothers,* consisting of all women in our congregation who wanted to sing together and share a message of love. Each singer dressed in a black skirt and white blouse for performances, and the harmony of angels filled our little chapel as their conductor directed them.

As a child, I couldn't help noticing that similarities of the women in our congregation ended with their black skirts and white blouses. *The Singing Mothers* came in all sizes and shapes. Some were crowned with halos of white hair, some had black, blonde, brown or grey hair. Some were sopranos, others altos. Those who were talented in music stood by those who needed help. No one had to audition. No one had to be popular or smart. No one had to qualify as a mother who had given birth. Every woman who wanted to participate could and did. The only requirements were black skirts, white blouses, willing hearts, and a commitment to follow the conductor.

As we listened to *The Singing Mothers,* I felt a spark that warmed my heart many times during my childhood. I wanted to grow up and join them. Alas, our family moved, and *The Singing Mothers* as defined above are now enshrined in memory and a favorite photo.

Now, I'm one of millions, maybe billions of women belonging to every faith and denomination. We look to God, our Divine Conductor, for guidance. With His help, we harmonize our efforts and talents on behalf of families from the smallest barrios to the largest cities, from parishes to palaces across the world.

SECTION 4

FAMILIES

I Believe in Families

I believe in families.

I believe in Crayons, blocks and Legos . . . and in PTA, putting them away.

I believe in chores and homework.

I believe in candy canes and M&M's.

I believe in drinking milk, brushing teeth, and reading bedtime stories.

I believe in training wheels and picnics.

I believe in Santa, the Easter Bunny, and the Tooth Fairy. One at a time.

I believe in sunscreen, freckles, and dentist appointments.

I believe in learning to make peanut butter sandwiches at an early age.

I believe in saying, *'I love you'* and *'I'm sorry'* . . . daily.

I believe in fixing meals, eating, and cleaning up after them . . . together.

I believe in birthday parties.

I believe in loving people as they are . . . including myself.

I believe in knowing brothers and sisters can be *'best friends'* from birth.

I believe in curfews and telling parents the truth, every time.

I believe in buying shoes, and more shoes, and then more shoes.

I believe in kneeling to teach a child how to tie shoes and how to pray.

I believe in Thanksgiving Dinner and ringing bells on New Year's Day.

I believe in stocking up on toilet tissue, shampoo and Kleenex.

I believe in attending band concerts, dance recitals, and soccer games.

I believe in parent-teacher conferences, book fairs, and carnivals.

I believe in Band-Aids and the power to '*kiss it better, Mommy!*'

I believe in summer vacations, trampolines, and swimming lessons.

I believe in going to church, reading The Bible, and making wise choices.

I believe in my parents, and in their parents, and even in their parents.

And I believe in home, because . . . I believe in families.

Where Seldom is Heard a
Discouraging Word

Not many families enjoy a *'Home on the Range'* setting, *'where seldom is heard a discouraging word, and the skies are not cloudy all day.'*

From the time a baby starts throwing Cheerios, toddling toward strange dogs, spitting food out and heading for electrical sockets, parents respond with, *'No, no!'* A certain amount of knee-jerk answers are required to keep children safe and their environment intact, but a constant clatter of negative responses can do damage.

Once, I heard a noisy mother berating her children in public. The children responded with blank faces and appeared deaf to her approach. When I got home, I started listening to myself talk to our children.

At first, I was encouraged. I wasn't labeling our children as lazy, stupid, clumsy or slow. I wasn't swearing, comparing their behavior to others or saying things like, *'You'll never amount to anything,'* or *'Why can't you be like your sister?'* I wasn't yelling, labeling or belittling, but I kept hearing myself use the word *'no'* and the negative contraction words, *can't, not, won't, shouldn't, couldn't and don't.*

I realized that a constant stream of negative contraction words is like a squeaky wheel, grating against the positive relationships I'm trying to build with family and friends. I decided to avoid those words when possible and use language patterns that encourage others . . . positively.

I started with a mind game. Every time I caught myself saying, *'no'* or one of the negative contraction words, *can't, not, don't, won't, couldn't, wouldn't, or shouldn't* in relation to behaviors, I tried to figure out afterward how I could have used '*can, will, shall, yes, could or do*' instead . . . next time.

For example:
1. When a child runs toward his bike without a helmet, just say, '*Remember to put your helmet on.*' It's a subtle difference from hollering, '*Don't get on that bike without your helmet!*' But which command would I rather receive?
2. A six-year-old asks if he can go out to play. I could say, '*Not until your bed is made,*' or, '*Yes you can, as soon as your bed is made.*'
3. Your baby reaches for the tube of lipstick in your purse. Instead of grabbing his hand and saying '*No, no,*' quickly exchange the lipstick for something else and say, '*Here you go!*'
4. Your teenager asks to use the car. Instead of, '*No. It's your night to do the dishes,*' say '*I'll help with the dishes so you can be home by 9:30.*'

I admit. The examples above are simplified. Incorporating this method into daily life is challenging and more than 1, 2, 3 and done. I thought chances for success would be slim. Yet, whenever I caught myself giving a snappy negative response, I challenged myself to redesign the words into ones of encouragement. It's actually not that hard to do.

Effective communication patterns take devotion and a marathon mentality, especially when schedules, surprises, interruptions and differences in maturity levels are constant. That said, it's worth the effort to stick with the goal of making our '*home on the range*' one where '*seldom is heard a discouraging word.*'

Story Problems

When I was in elementary school, we had a subject called Arithmetic.

At the beginning of each lesson, our teacher introduced a new numbers concept related to adding, subtracting, multiplying or dividing. Each new concept was followed by an assignment. We copied the problems from our Arithmetic books onto a blank sheet of paper, figured out how to solve them, and wrote our answers below or beside each problem. Easy.

But . . . at the end of each lesson, 'story problems' loomed in dense and heavy sentences and paragraphs that awaited us like a pond of lazy alligators lurking under the surface, just waiting to snatch our confidence — and even our recess! Nobody liked story problems. Even our Arithmetic teacher didn't like them! It helped to read the story problems out loud in class, then try to solve them together, but it was never fun.

The one nice thing about solving Arithmetic problems was that each problem had only one right answer. Even story problems written in long paragraphs had only one right answer. Besides, our teacher, who knew everything about Arithmetic, had a handy 'answer key" in the back of her book nearby, just in case nobody could figure out how to get the answer.

In the school for solving problems at home, it might be fairly easy to memorize the basic principles of love, devotion, kindness and generosity.

But mastering the endless varieties of *story problems* that come up any and every day in a family — gets messy. There may even be different *'right answers'* for every single family member! So how does all that *add up*?

Well . . . that's a different kind of story problem.

SECTION 5

FOOD

Families Gotta Eat!

When my parents got married in 1936, they pooled their money with two other couples and bought a cow. The husbands worked out a schedule for milking the cow and sharing the milk and cream.

Three times a day, my parents gathered around a meal that Mother had planned and prepared from scratch. When the meal was over, she washed and dried every dish by hand and began thinking about what to prepare for the next meal.

Mother repeated this process for her husband and family for over sixty years! Let's see, that's 3 meals a day, times 365 days a year, times 60 years equals 65,700 meals! Who knew?

In those 'olden days,' family mealtime around the table was a life-sustaining habit. It was a time for the family to gather, eat, talk, plan, share, laugh, decide and pray . . . together. The general rule was that you were there, at the table, at a specific time, or you missed out!

Fast food, microwaves, dishwashers and crazy schedules have changed everything about mealtime. One stubborn fact remains. Hunger is as predictable as the sunrise and more frequent. Families gotta eat!

While meal prep and cleanup have gotten easier, meeting regularly as a family is much more challenging. My guess is that nobody wants to return to plucking feathers from chickens, baking bread and churning butter as necessary rituals for preparing a nourishing meal. That said, families need to figure out ways for modern time-savers to unite family members rather than divide them.

As I was writing this article, three of our boys gathered around a bowl of popcorn discussing which person had a bigger impact on history, Marilyn Monroe or Ghandi.

Really? Are you kidding? No. I'm really not.

Still . . . it was three brothers, eating and sharing ideas and attitudes around a bowl of popcorn with best friends, whose opinions they respect and care about. Regardless of which boy's ideas prevail, their circle of debate reminds me that enjoying food together as a family is a winning recipe in any era . . . even when it's just one kernel of unity at a time.

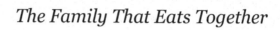

The Family That Eats Together

Psychologists say families who eat together have a winning edge in the real world. I suppose that could be true. This is how it went at the table when our daughter and son-in-law brought our grandchildren for dinner:

Grandpa (my husband, Dan): *'Who's up for a round of golf?'*
Randy (son-in-law): *'I didn't bring my clubs.'*
Anthony (age 21): *'I have a date. Sorry, Dad.'*
Rachel (age 6*): 'Mommy, Dart (age 3) is playing in his water.'*
Grandma (me): *'Please pass the meat pie.'*
Jill (our daughter, the mommy): *'Rachel, do we tattle in our family?'*
Rachel: *'But Mommy, he IS playing in his water.'*
Jill: *'Thank you, Rachel. Dart, keep your hands out of the water.'*
Grandma: ***'Please** pass the meat pie.'*
Janette (age 15): *'Mom, can I clean my room tomorrow instead?'*
Ethan (age 18): "*Aren't we supposed to pass food to the right?'*
Rachel: *'Mommy, he's doing it again, and he's gargling, too.'*
Jill: *'Dart, keep your hands out of the water or you won't **have** water.*
Grandma: *'I'd **really** like a bite of that meat pie before it's all gone.'*
Jill: *'Dart, eat your meat pie . . . and no more bubbles.'*
Dart: *'Grandma, can I have a cereal bar?'*
Jill: *'If you're hungry enough for a cereal bar, you're hungry enough to finish your meat pie.'*
Rachel: *'Mommy, Dart spilled his water!"*

Jill: *'So, he can clean it up.'*
Dart: *'Grandma, can I have a woffcloff?'*
Grandma: *'I'll trade you a woffcloff for a bite of your meat pie!'*

On second thought, I think the psychologists have a point.

Popcorn Makes a House a Home

There's been some discussion about what makes a house a home. Some say a house becomes a home when it's decorated just right. Others say a family has to live in a house for a certain amount of time before it's a real home. Actually, the real test is popcorn.

You won't find a real home that can't prove it with popcorn because the only people who don't love popcorn are people who are attached to braces. They hate popcorn because they love it so much that when they see it, they're reminded they can't have any until the braces come off. The first thing they eat on the day the wires are removed is a bowl of caramel popcorn.

A real home has popcorn in all the usual places — under the beds, in between the sofa cushions, and in the silverware drawer. The homiest homes go a little further. They have *'old maids'* inside the light fixtures, in a bottle of mouthwash, in a brown paper bag that's hiding in the dryer, mixed into the jar of "creamy" peanut butter by the child who prefers his peanut butter to be *'chunky,'* and taped to the refrigerator door to resemble a cherry tree in bloom. Don't ask me how I know this.

Popcorn does magical things to a house. The smell of it sends this message: Come on in . . . loosen your tie . . . you're home now . . . pull out the games . . . take your shoes off . . . no worries . . . relax.

For every house transformed into a home by popcorn, there's a price to be paid called *'the morning after.'* Most mothers are familiar with the person who pays that price. Out comes the vacuum, the *'Glass Plus'* and the broom. Wipe buttery fingerprints from the TV, walls and windows. Gather bowls and salt shakers. Then, go straight to the mirror and promise yourself you won't allow your house to be turned into a home again . . . for a whole week.

Please Pass the Tradition

My Grandma Price bought the set of pastel pink *'Daileyware'* for our family of eight in the 50's, when my brothers and sisters and I were children. The place setting for six included dinner plates, medium-size lunch plates, tumblers, cups and saucers, soup and cereal bowls. Each piece was crafted out of a light, indestructible material that never cracked or chipped and was supposed to last forever.

Our Thomas Family rule was to be prompt for dinner, which was served *'family style'* around the table and set with the *'Daileyware'* at 6:00 p.m. Sharp.

Granted, there were a few exceptions. On Thanksgiving Day, Christmas and New Year's, we might use Mother's fancy china. On the Fourth of July, we used paper plates for a picnic. We sometimes went camping or on trips to visit Grandma Price, leaving the neat stacks of *'Daileyware'* at home in the cupboard, behind closed doors.

The 60's passed, then the 70's and the 80's. The *'Daileyware'* was used hundreds of times, thousands, then who knows how many more times? My siblings and I grew up, left home, married and had families of our own, but we always found our way back home to Mom, Dad and the *'Daileyware.'*

In the early 90's, our oldest brother presented our parents with a new set of dishes. They were brown. Plain. They had no white speckles. They were heavy. *'Stoneware.'* Dishes. Our brother told our Mother that the *'Daileyware'* was outdated. Then, he went so far as to hint that he had never enjoyed eating from pink dishes that had white speckles on them.

When the heavy, brown *'Stoneware'* dishes were introduced to our family, the reaction of our siblings, their spouses and twenty-five grandchildren was swift and unanimous. Eating Grandma's homemade meals from anything but pink *'Daileyware'* with white speckles was boring and against our family code of conduct.

Always the peacemaker, Grandma asked Kim, the granddaughter who majored in art, to take the six pink dinner plates and paint a traditional Thomas *'reminder meal'* on each one. So that's what Kim did.

At our parents' 61st wedding anniversary celebration, each family was presented with a personalized *'Daileyware'* dinner plate. The plates are now proudly displayed in prominent places in our homes.

As for the heavy *'Stoneware'* dishes, they make a sturdy stack of brown in our mother's cupboard for the medium-sized *'Daileyware'* supper plates to nest in between meals. That way, they'll be on top and can be used by Grandpa and Grandma for breakfast, dinner and supper meals.

Since family members visit in small batches these days, there are usually enough medium-sized *'Daileyware'* plates to go around, and everyone is happy.

One thing is certain. This set of pastel pink with white speckles *'Daileyware,'* was crafted out of an indestructible material that never cracks or chips and is supposed to last forever.

It probably will.

---

* This article was written in the 1990's. Mother washed and dried every dirty dish by hand and never owned an 'automatic' dishwasher. When asked why she didn't ask her children to help with the dishes more often, she said that doing the dishes gave her a chance to have a little time to herself. Our parents invested in a microwave oven later, which made meal prep and clean-up much easier for them.

SECTION 6

GRANDPARENTS

Oops!

I'm in trouble with my daughter, Jill. At least, I'm not the only one. The other grandma is in trouble, too.

Both of us live in Boise, and we took care of our grandchildren, Rachel (age 5) and Dart (age 2) while Jill filled her assignment as a youth group leader last week.

I guess we went a little overboard keeping our grandchildren happy. Like we don't have excuses! For one thing, they're the first grandchildren on both sides, and we don't get to see them often. I guess we got a bit confused about some of the rules.

We had to let them stay up after bedtime because, when we told Dart it was time to go to bed, he turned to us and said, *"No tank you, Gamma."* A little boy with such good manners needs positive reinforcement, don't you think?

We didn't want leftover cookies after the grandchildren had gone home, so we let them eat as many as they wanted. We were allowing them to have their own way when they asked for whatever because, honestly, we were trying to make up for all the mean things we did to their parents when they were kids. Besides, we didn't want to hear them cry.

Not only that, over the years, our own children trained us to pick up after them, so we didn't know our grandchildren are supposed to pick up after themselves.

I suppose we spoiled them a little. But it was just one week! Now, they don't want to follow the *'old rules'* of their mean parents. What can we say? We were just following the bad examples of our own mothers when they were behaving like grandmas.

Grandmas Ask 'Why Not?'

I thought I knew my sister, Karen. That was before she became the grandmother of two little girls, Chase and Kambria.

I thought my sister, Karen's favorite activity was shopping.

Then why is she giving up an afternoon at the Mall in favor of babysitting?

I thought my sister, Karen's idea of clutter was a stray carrot peel in the sink. Then why are toys and stuffed animals scattered all over the floor in her living room?

My sister, Karen always looks like she just stepped out of a fashion magazine. Then why are grass stains on her jeans and bits of twigs sticking out of her hair from rolling down the hill at the park?

My sister, Karen takes pride in her nails, which are always manicured and polished. Then why is she in the backyard helping Chase knead the dough for mud pies?

My sister, Karen takes excellent care of her belongings and never damages property. Then why did she admit that she can't turn Chase down when Chase appears out of nowhere with a sparkle in her eyes and says, *"Gammy . . . let's go jump on your bed!"*

My sister, Karen taught home economics for over thirty years and owns organizational skills and habits galore. Then why are snacking and playing with Chase and Kambria her only accomplishments today?

I thought I knew my sister, Karen.

Now, I'm kind of glad I didn't.

I guess she's just like the rest of us who have spent years coping with the question, *"Why?"*

When grandchildren come into our lives, it's just a lot more fun to ask, *"Why not?"*

About Rectangular Grandmas

It's amazing what parents learn when *they* listen, and their *children* talk. Years ago, when our house was brimming with preschoolers, I took notes when the topic of a *'family home evening'* discussion was grandmas. Here are some observations our kids made that I shared later with their grandmothers, Verla Thomas and Ellen Hawkley:

"We drive way past a nap to get to Grandma's house. We're lucky our grandmas live in the same town. When we get there, we go in without knocking. First, they give us kisses and long hugs."

"Grandma Hawkley calls our Dad, *'Dan'* and tells him to put a coat on to go outside. We look at each other and laugh, because nobody else tells our dad what to do!"

"Grandma plays *'olden-days'* songs on a fiddle and helps us put on our shoes with a spoon just like the one the shoe store guy has."

"Grandmas like to make picnics. They grow dill pickles and peas and tomatoes in their gardens. They can make fruit leather out of anything! They make soup out of *'rolling pin noodles.'* They put better stuff in Jello. Grandma Thomas can even make a cake out of a zucchini!"

"Grandmas have good laps. They have time to read two stories in a row. When they take a nap with me, they don't get up in the middle."

"Grandmas have new sheets. They bring me more blankets so I won't get cold. In the morning, they make my bed and tell me not to wake up my mom."

"When you break Grandma's lamp, she just buys a new one and asks you to be more careful."

"Grandmas like to play checkers even when I always win. They pick up our toys and gives us quarters to buy candy at the little store."

"When we go home, our grandmas are sad, but they send food with us so we won't get hungry on the way."

"Grandmas look . . . something like a rectangle. They have soft hair and sparkling eyes with glasses on them. Their faces are a little *'folded.'* Some other grandmas have purple hair, but not ours."

Hmmmmm. Now that I'm a grandma myself, I'm happy to report that recognizing grandmas has changed, but come to think of it, not that much. So, if you meet up with a rectangle who has sparkly eyes and likes playing checkers with preschoolers, never fear.

It's just somebody's grandma.

Beatitudes for Grandparents

Blessed are those who have wrinkly smiles:
for their eyes twinkle.
Blessed are those with more than one chin:
for their tummies jiggle when they laugh.
Blessed are those who cannot hear what is said:
for they listen with their hearts.
Blessed are those with crooked fingers:
for their touch is gentle.
Blessed are those with white hair:
for they have the halos of angels.
Blessed are the poor in dollars and cents:
for they share jewels of character.
Blessed are those who remain silent about their pain:
for they shall not be one.
Blessed are those whose brains are slow to remember:
for their mouths are first to forgive.
Blessed are those whose bodies are worn out:
for their spirits are worn in.
Rejoice, and be exceeding glad:
for great is the reward of those who joyfully lay aside
the titles of 'Mom and Dad' in gratitude
for their legacy as 'Grand' and 'Great-Grand' parents.

"I asked Heavenly Father
to mend the world...
and He sent one carpenter."

HOLIDAYS

An Optimist's Thanksgiving

I have many things to be grateful for on Thanksgiving, starting with these ten:

1. I'm thankful to be an optimist. It means I look forward with confidence.
2. I'm thankful for a counter covered with dirty dishes. It means all of us left the table with full stomachs.
3. I'm thankful a new bill makes its way to our mailbox each month. It means our new gas furnace is doing its job.
4. I'm thankful for piles of leaves in our yard. It means we had shade in summer and a fun 'wake-up-rake-up' day ahead.
5. I'm thankful for news anchors, weather forecasters, politicians and actors. It means when I'm tired of news, views and entertainment, I turn them off.
6. I'm thankful for piles of laundry in the laundry room. It means I have hot and cold running water and a magic washer / dryer combo.
7. I'm thankful to live in America. It means I have the right to vote and a legacy of 'liberty and justice' for all.
8. I'm thankful for friends, family and strangers whose looks, thoughts and actions are different from my own. It means the world is always fascinating.
9. I'm thankful for several pairs of shoes strewn around the family room. It means our family attended church together. And . . .
10. I'm thankful that God gave us 10 commandments instead of 10 suggestions. It means there's no question about what 'to do' and 'not to do' to be happy.

About the Sweet Potatoes

I never met a Thanksgiving I didn't like. I like the turkey, homemade rolls and pumpkin pie. I like the family gatherings and watching the Macy's Thanksgiving Day Parade. I even like the football games. I like everything, except . . . maybe the sweet potatoes. We have them even though nobody eats them because, it's Thanksgiving!

Thanksgiving is about tradition, counting our blessings and our heritage as Americans, which began in 1620, when William Bradford and his little band of English castoffs made the two-month voyage across the Atlantic Ocean searching for religious freedom and a new life. Sick and exhausted, they landed at Plymouth Rock in December and were forced to spend much of the winter on the Mayflower. Half of them died. In the spring, friendly natives, led by Chief Massosoit, rescued them by teaching them how to hunt, fish and grow native crops. In the fall of 1621, those who survived hosted the first Thanksgiving feast of wild turkey, venison, pumpkin pie, vegetables, oysters, clams and bread.

I'm not proud of how Massosoit's descendants were ultimately thanked for extending their hospitality. It's not a secret that American history is checkered with imperfections to this day.

Still, we as Americans proudly sing, *'This land is your land, this land is my land.'* But Massasoit was right. This land belongs to the Great Spirit. The bounties that come from America are products of His creation and His generosity, not ours. It's our job to appreciate those creations, to participate in the good and foster the better.

Three cheers for Thanksgiving! Here's to stuffing the turkey and ourselves! Here's to talking to and feasting with relatives and friends. Here's to all of us, pausing to thank God. And last of all . . . here's to the sweet potatoes!

About the Sweet Potatoes: Round Two

A favorite thing about writing is feedback from friends and even a few strangers. One November, I wrote a Thanksgiving article that took a cheap shot at sweet potatoes. The reason I served them for Thanksgiving had everything to do with tradition and nothing to do with my family's taste buds. Evidently, making a statement like that borders on being un-American. Who knew?

Fortunately, my friend, Bonnie, sent a sweet potatoes recipe that got rave reviews in our family, where servings of sweet potatoes had previously been scooped onto plates by the half-teaspoon.

So . . . here it is . . . presenting . . . the updated Thanksgiving recipe tradition.

It's calorie and cholesterol free . . . NOT. But hey, it's Thanksgiving. We can retreat to *'Eat until you're full, but only on Thanksgiving'* . . . tomorrow.

Sweet Potato Soufflé

6 cups cooked and mashed sweet potatoes
1 1/2 cups sugar
1 teaspoon salt
1/2 cup butter (not margarine)
4 eggs
1 cup evaporated milk
2 teaspoons vanilla

Bake three large sweet potatoes in 350 degree oven for two hours or until soft. Peel jackets off. Combine above ingredients in mixer and mix until light and fluffy. Pour into 9x13 inch pan that has been sprayed with Pam.

Topping

1 cup brown sugar
1/3 cup flour
1 cup chopped pecans
1/2 cup melted butter (not margarine)
1/3 cup coconut

Mix ingredients together and sprinkle over sweet potato mixture. Bake @ 350 degrees for 40 minutes. Enjoy!

The Christmas Rocker

December always bullies its way into my life. When holiday events and lists start to scramble my brain, I recall a simpler Christmas . . . our first Christmas together as husband and wife . . . the year of the rocker.

Our financial situation was bleak in December of 1967 as we juggled college courses at BYU, part-time jobs and our uncharted status as expectant parents.

By late November, I was eight months pregnant and exhausted. All I wanted for Christmas was for our baby to arrive, but Dan was bent on displaying his Prince Charming talents. He claimed a small tree that had been abandoned on the curb after semester break, concocted a tree stand from a discarded angel food cake pan, and crafted strings of popcorn, construction paper chains and egg shell *'balls.'* Instead of a star, a cloud of cotton cradled a tiny angel, the symbol of our baby's safe arrival.

We were sure my swollen frame would deliver its burden before Christmas, but alas, the flashing holiday lights along our street on Christmas Eve stopped blinking abruptly, so we gave up and went to bed. We awoke on Christmas morning realizing that the gift no material trimming could match would not be delivered that day. I rolled out of bed and tottered toward the kitchen, glancing at the Christmas tree in our tiny living room and beheld a beautiful wooden rocker! The baby hadn't come, but suddenly, *'out of the blue,'* we were furniture owners! On the back of the rocker, Santa had left a message:

*"The chair is to my sweetheart, and to my baby, too.
In fact, we all will use it whenever we feel blue;
We'll rock away our troubles and laugh away our tears,
And fill our lives with bubbles as we rock away the years."*

We paid for the rocker in six installments of $5. each . . . but it wasn't the rocker or the lengthy payments that locked the Christmas of 1967 into my memory bank. It was anticipating the birth of our first child, who would turn the three of us into a family.

Every Christmas has been different for our family since then, but the message of Christmas remains the same:

*"For God so loved the world, that he gave his only
begotten Son, that whosoever believeth in him
should not perish, but have everlasting life."
John 3:16*

Christmas, When Everything
Didn't Get Done

One blustery twenty-fourth night in December,
Time's candle had snuffed, leaving nary an ember;
I lay in my bed knowing all was not right,
Christmas would come at the first break of light.

The cards were not sent, and the pies were not ready,
A burden much worse made my heartbeat unsteady;
No gifts had been bought for each daughter and son,
Christmas . . . when everything didn't get done.

My pillow was crumpled and stained with fresh tears,
I felt all alone with my fate and my fears;
I wondered how God would approach such a trial
And awake in the morning still wearing a smile.

Then, amidst my emotion, a single thought stirred,
It fluttered and gently alit like a bird;
God, in His infinite, wonderful way
Had left out so much on that first Christmas Day!

He left out the gingerbread and fruitcake making;
In fact, he left out all the holiday baking.
He left out the candy canes, chestnuts and eggnog;
He left out the turkey, the toffee and Yule log.

He left out the good cheer of 'Frosty' and snow,
He left out the wreaths and the warm fire's glow.

He left out the ornaments, parties and pageants,
He left out the toys that each young child imagines.

Instead of the pomp and the trimmings and trappings,
Instead of the presents in colorful wrappings;
God offered His gift from an animal's stall,
Wrapped in crude bands and a young mother's shawl.

Just one little baby, so gentle and mild,
A common occurrence, the birth of a child;
Yet with this special baby, salvation was won,
For God so loved the world that He gave His own Son!

I knew in that moment that all would be well,
Christmas would come with its usual spell;
I could survive without even one elf,
I could give presents right out of myself!

And so, Christmas morning, the family awoke,
We laughed and we played even though we were broke;
With plenty to eat, we were warm and content,
Our happiness seemed, for the most, heaven sent.

And so I suggest, if you're ever in doubt,
And need to know what Christmas fuss is about;
Reach deep inside you and pull out your best,
Give something better than toys or a vest.

Give something meaningful, something unique,
It may be as small as the words that you speak.
You'll find, if you do, that when Christmas is past
You have given a gift like God's Son, that will last.

The Family Heirloom

While Christmas shopping, my friend, Dawn Johnson, bought an expensive manger scene that was on sale for $29.95. Of course, her little daughter, Breanna, wanted to play with the breakable figurines. Another *'of course'* is that Dawn tried to teach Breanna to avoid playing with them.

All Dawn's efforts to keep the set *'nice'* went unheeded. Dawn's mother reminded her how she had felt while visiting her own Grandma's' house as a little girl, where the atmosphere was often tense, and touching *'valuables'* was strictly forbidden.

"For heaven's sakes," her mother pleaded, *"let Breanna PLAY! After all . . . for $29.95 . . . this creche is NOT a family heirloom!'"*

Good point. From that day, the manger scene saw a lot of action from Breanna and her friends. A careful investigation shows evidence that each piece has been repaired time after time. If figurines could talk, each could tell stories of adventures that happened at the hands of little children at play.

"This scar is where my leg got broken off while I was trying to kneel by the manger," a shepherd might say.

"This is where my wings got clipped that time I was flying too close to the fireplace," an angel might add.

Mary might reflect, *"This is where Baby Jesus got his paint rubbed off from having the swaddling clothes smoothed so much."*

This Christmas, the manger scene has taken its usual place in the Johnson household. Recently, Dawn's mother stopped by and suggested that it might be a good year to look for a new manger scene to replace the well-seasoned one.

Dawn's reaction was swift and sure. *"Mom! Are you kidding? We'll NEVER part with this set! Do you have ANY idea how many times I've glued these figures back together? Breanna has been playing with this manger scene since she was a little girl. Why . . . it's a . . . **a family heirloom!**"*

A Thomas Christmas Story

My favorite Christmas story is in the Bible about how Jesus was born. It's short to read and long to think about. I like the part where ordinary angels and shepherds get to do the important job of welcoming baby Jesus since, as everyone knows, Jesus isn't the least bit ordinary.

My second favorite Christmas story is in my Aunt Margaret's journal. The star of the story is her dad, my Grandpa Thomas, who got to do something important one Christmas, even though he was as ordinary as the shepherds.

That Christmas, my Aunt Margaret was a young girl with freckles and long, red hair as fluffy as yarn. Grandpa Thomas was young in dad years, too. Back then, the Thomas family didn't have electric lights, but nobody else did, either. Their Christmas tree was decorated with paper chains, strings of popcorn and candleholders that held little candles that were real.

"When can we light the tree?" Margaret and her siblings asked every night as the family gathered after supper in the parlor. *"We can't wait!"*

Finally, the long-awaited night arrived. *"We were told to stay far back while Dad and Mother lit each little candle. After all the candles had been lit, "everybody 'oh'd and ah'ed' at the tree's beauty."* Aunt Margaret began to dance around the tree in excitement. In a sudden burst of energy, she whirled around, and one of the tiny flames caught her long red hair, lighting her head on fire.

Just as suddenly, my ordinary Grandpa rushed to her side as his two big hands came down on her head again and again until the fire was put out. Then, he gathered Margaret up into his sturdy arms, held her close and wept. Grandma Thomas quickly put out the other flickering candles on the tree while Grandpa comforted Margaret in the big rocking chair.

That year, Christmas Day came like it always does. It took time for Margaret's beautiful red hair to grow in again and for Grandpa's hands to heal. But that didn't matter. They had plenty of time. A loving father had reached out to rescue his daughter, even though she had made a mistake, just like God did in the Bible when He reached out to rescue His children by sending Jesus to rescue all of us from ours.

It's short to read, but long to think about.

Peace on Earth

Rulers and presidents promise it.
Children wish for it.
Parents yearn for it.
Choirs sing of it.
Philosophers study it.
Historians speak of it.
Poets write about it.
Sinners pray for it.
Soldiers die in the name of it.
The sun, the moon and the stars reflect it,
And all creation is drawn to it.
But only One has the power,
The majesty and the meekness
To offer it with these words . . .
"Peace I leave with you,
my peace I give unto you;
not as the world giveth,
give I unto you.
let not your heart be troubled,
neither let it be afraid."
Jesus.
The babe, the son of Mary.
The light and the life of the world.
The Prince of Peace.

John 14:27

This Very Christmas . . .

I shall be a carpenter who shelters
a cherished one from a tide of scorn . . .
I shall be a donkey that carries the burden
of a fellow traveler on a far journey . . .
I shall be an innkeeper
who has room in the inn . . .
I shall be a servant who hears the muffled cries
of a frightened young mother and hastens to her aid . . .
I shall be an angel who joins with a multitude of
the Heavenly host, praising God and singing,
'*Joy to the world, the Lord is come!*' . . .
I shall be a humble shepherd whose ears are
first to hear good tidings of great joy . . .
I shall be a mother who tenderly cradles
the treasure of eternity . . .
I shall be a noble wise man who follows the star
to kneel before the manger of an infant king . . .
And this very Christmas . . .
I shall be a child of God who, with hope, wraps the gift
of peace on earth and gently places its fragile contents
beneath the Christmas tree of humanity.

SECTION 8

LITERACY & TRADITIONS

In the Middle of Rumpelstiltskin

I phoned my friend, Delma Atwell. She said she would get back to me. She was *'right in the middle of Rumpelstiltskin'* with her boys, Tim and Ted, and couldn't be interrupted.

I admit. I was jealous. Her words transported me to the hours my children nestled on either side of me, eagerly anticipating every word of a favorite story. But, alas and alack . . . all my *'Tims and Teds'* have been independent readers for years and have no use for the lullaby of bedtime stories.

Our collection of worn-and-torn childhood favorites rests behind closed doors in the hall closet, waiting for grandchildren to visit. Among them are books my children loved most; *Marvin K. Mooney Will You Please Go Now, The Poky Little Puppy, Ferdinand the Bull,* and *The Cat in the Hat,* for starters.

I recall the feeling of safety and wonder as my own mother sat between my siblings and me reading *The Teeny Tiny Lady, The Three Little Pigs,* and many more.

Did I read to my children enough? That depends. How much is enough? I tried to read to them every day, but I didn't always succeed. All of them are good readers, if that's the point, but fostering a love for reading isn't the sole objective of reading together. Perhaps it isn't possible to read to a child *'enough.'*

I'd like to go back and hear the rhythm of my mother's voice as she read the familiar *'once upon a times'* and *'happily ever afters.'* I'd like to go back and hear my children correct me whenever I skipped a word or two of a favorite book.

What I know is this. You can talk to friends or finish the laundry or work on your list of things to do any day, because you can always come back to friends and laundry and lists. They always wait. But children don't stay children. They grow up and move away.

If wishes came true like they sometimes do in books, I would wish that I had never been *'too busy'* to read to our children.

Not 'The End'

Dedicated readers never want their journey with words to end. My mother was one of those people, a prolific reader and writer who wrote letters to each of her six children every Sunday for over forty years. If we hadn't received our letter from Mother by Wednesday, we knew it was because a holiday had interrupted their delivery, not that our mother had neglected to write or mail her letters.

One letter I recall in particular, written when Mother was in her 90s, included a recipe for sauerkraut that she copied from one of the books in the *Dear America* series. According to Mother, the recipe described the way her parents made sauerkraut in the early 1900's. I think she wanted me to make some.

I was glad I had paid attention to Mrs. Stuart, my 4th grade teacher, who taught me about fractions and division, because the first item on the recipe was 15 heads of cabbage. The recipe also called for a huge barrel (*'scrubbed, scalded and set in the sun to dry'*), a board across two chairs, and a sharp knife. Then, as if the instructions weren't exhilarating enough already—I was supposed to enlist the help of *'Stanley'* after I had *'helped him with his bath and spent extra time cleaning his feet, for it is the husband's job to tamp the cabbage.'* Well, that complicated things, since I don't know anyone by the name of Stanley and am not interested in finding one.

If you guessed that our mother's love of reading ignited many an adventure in her life and the lives of her children, you would be right.

Who could forget snuggling on either side of her, waiting for *The Teeny, Tiny Lady* in the storybook to yell, *'Take it!'* after the hidden voice that was coming from her teeny tiny cupboard demanded in a loud, then louder, then the loudest voice, *'Give me my bone!'* Mother's flair for drama and her inflections while reading that story nearly scared our freckles off, but we never tired of that story and asked her to read it again and again.

The literacy journey Mother inspired in her children continues on in her posterity. The way I see it, endless flights of history, fiction, adventure, mystery and non-fiction begin on a runway of black and white, then pick up speed and take to the skies toward entertainment, relaxation, learning, adventure and word travel.

Our mother was that rare individual who finished what she started. When she broke her right wrist, she decided, in her 80's, to learn how to write with her left hand so that she could continue writing letters to her children. Her letters were shorter, but we still received them every week. She finished what she started until *'The End.'*

*Note: My mother, Verla Thomas, passed away in 2008, leaving a legacy of letters, the love of music, macaroni and cheese and a great family. I miss her every day, but recognize her special brand of love every time I meet with one of my siblings or any of her 25 grandchildren. P.S. In case you're interested, the sauerkraut I made from the recipe Mom sent was delicious, even though I had to settle for a stainless steel knife, a sturdy wooden spoon, a couple of Pyrex dishes, and, in the absence of Stanley, a moderately effective dishwasher.

To Hug Or Not To Hug?

People are either huggers or not. I'm a hugger, but I try to keep my preference in check.

I've noticed non-huggers are gaining in their effort to convert us huggers. There are new non-hugging rules, written and unwritten.

It's a good idea to figure those rules out before making an innocent mistake. It can be tricky.

Take football players for example. They're mostly big, proud, powerful, mean-looking, competitive non-huggers. But, who are they kidding? I've watched them operate. After one of them makes a big play, the biggest, proudest, most powerful, meanest-looking, most competitive non-hugging football players come charging each other at full speed, butting their heads together . . . and hugging!

Just between you and me, I like to ask the person I want to hug before *'going for it'* just to be on the safe side.

The top ten reasons for hugging are:

1. A hug is free.
2. A hug takes only five seconds from start to finish.
3. A hug can make people feel warm and accepted.
4. A hug says, *'You and I are on the same team.'*
5. A hug speaks every language, nationality, size, age, color or creed.
6. A hug has no calories.
7. A hug requires no preparation.
8. A hug is a gift given and a gift received at the same time.
9. A hug can become a treasured memory.
10. A hug says, *"I care about you."*

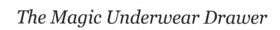

The Magic Underwear Drawer

I heard about the magic underwear drawer from a friend who has one. Every morning, as he opens the drawer, neatly folded stacks of clean underwear appear as if by magic. This has been going on at his house for decades without a hint of interruption.

Some may say that a magic underwear drawer is more valuable than the expensive contracts of the Tooth Fairy, the Easter Bunny and Santa Claus combined, but a bill or request for compensation has never been presented.

Suppliers of magic underwear drawers seem to be a rather shy bunch. To my knowledge, they've never lobbied for a title. Let's see. *Fairy Godmother, Tinkerbell, The Angel of Mercy* and *Mother Teresa* are already taken.

But wait. Not so fast.

Now that I think of it, those of us who participate in the successful operation of magic underwear drawers may also be drivers who go to work, do errands and attend endless events, but never need to stop at a gas station since, for some reason, the gas tank is always at least half full.

It's magic how that happens.

What Does 'I Love You' Mean?

I suppose a version of 'I love you' is spoken in every language worldwide.

But what does this simple message mean in any number of scenarios, and why is it a treasured gem of communication?

Maybe it's because:

'I love you' can mean:

I want you to be happy.

You're one of my favorites.

I think of you when we're apart and wonder how your day is going.

I want what's best for you and will help you achieve it.

You are on my 'first things first' list.

I take pride in your accomplishments.

I want to help you rebound from failures.

I will listen to your opinions when they are different from mine.

I won't shut you out when we can't agree.

'I love you' can mean:

The sound of your laughter puts me in a good mood.

I'm happy when we spend time together.

I like to plan and go on vacations with you.

I like to watch you do something spectacular or ordinary.

You never have to win first place.

I cry with you when you 'goof up' and don't keep track of them.

I'll never give up on you.

We share memories, birthday celebrations and toothpaste.
I'll say *'No'* to you when what you want may hurt you or others.

'I love you' can mean:
We hug each other and sometimes catch the same colds.
I appreciate and accept our differences and similarities.
I never want you to be hurt, afraid or alone.
I enjoy talking to you and being with you.
You don't have to be beautiful, famous, smart, healthy or wealthy.
When I look at you, I see what's on the inside first.
I always want you to succeed.
I pray for you every day.
I loved you *then,* I love you *now,* and I will love you *always.*

'I love you' can mean that we are connected *forever.*

Be a Cork

Recently, I reviewed a speech by Richard G. Scott, a wise religious leader. His topic was *'Finding Joy In Life.'* He suggested that, *"Some people are like rocks thrown into a sea of problems. They are drowned by them. Be a cork. When submerged in a problem, fight to be free, to bob up, to serve again with happiness."*

This analogy fits parents who, by the very nature of their work, must travel on a river of shallow and deep water, changing currents, twists and turns, unpredictable weather, even dramatic rapids. As problems arise, it's tempting to get weighed down like the flat rock that skips across the surface of the lake a few times when tossed by an expert, then settles into the security of a dark, but safe and secure river bed.

Some parents approach challenges like sponges that are cast upon a river and float lightheartedly along for a time. They have a desire to *'fit in'* with whatever the river dictates, but start soaking up more water than they can carry. Eventually, they become swamped and swallowed by the very elements they were attempting to please.

Then, there are parents who are corks. They travel the same river, but are buoyant and light-hearted. Strong currents may pull them under from time to time as they travel in rain, snow, wind, ice, sunshine and shade. Yet, they always pop up, travel with the river's flow and adapt to whatever changes happen with unsinkable courage and resilience. They remain constant to eternal principles, knowing God is in their DNA, keeping them on top of circumstances they may face, *no matter what.*

I'm privileged to have some of those young and old *'corks'* as my dear friends and want to be just like them.

SECTION 9

PARENTING

Confessions of an Amateur Parent

Before I was a parent, I was convinced that parenting wasn't *'rocket science.'*
For starters, I thought:

1. I had life figured out.
2. I already knew how to be a *'good'* parent.
3. I had the right answers to any child's question.
4. I was good at organizing.
5. Parents always know best.
6. My kids would be a lot like me.
7. Every child needs to take piano lessons.
8. I would never yell.
9. I would be finished parenting when all my kids had reached the age of 18.
10. I would be a perfect parent by now.

After decades in this business, I'm more convinced than ever that parenting isn't *'rocket science.'* That's because rocket scientists get to go home at night after ten-or-so hours of work, compared to the ups and downs, the whirls and swirls that occur in the world of parenting 24/7/52/365, from the day we learn *'we're pregnant'* to our very, very last breaths. The parenting journey includes surprises, growth, joy, sorrow, and the unimaginable adventures of a lifetime. And the most surprising confession of all? I never want them to end.

Parenting Is an Enigma

According to the dictionary, the word *'enigma'* means *'an obscure riddle.'* Parents are famous for being in the middle of them. For example, pregnant women are often delighted about *'having a baby,'* but not so excited about *'labor and delivery.'* Do they really want to give birth . . . or not? It's an enigma.

Parents are eager to begin the tasks of cuddling their infant, taking photos, learning about the baby's unique personality and introducing their little one to friends and family, but not so eager about morning, noon, and nighttime feedings, and of course, changing diapers. It's an enigma.

Parents can't wait to help their children learn to walk, knowing full well that a walking child turns into a running child whose main goal is often to run away from parents! Meanwhile, parents persist in offering boxes of crayons to children who find it more interesting to draw on large, white pieces of wall than on small, white pieces of paper. It's an enigma.

Parents pay for baseball coaches, piano lessons, orthodontists and debate team fees, knowing full well their signatures on the dotted line commit them to attending an infinite number of games, recitals, appointments and tournaments. That's an enigma if ever there was one!

Parents send their teenagers to driver's ed classes realizing the teenager will want a set of keys to the family car and any other slightly accessible vehicles the moment after the driver's ed certificate has been delivered into their hands. This is an enigma of substantial proportions!

Why are parents enthused about getting through the present stage so they can reap the uncharted territory of the next stage that has even more challenging consequences? There might be an answer to this question, but in a paragraph or two? Not so much.

All I know is that before long, parents are seated high in the bleachers of an auditorium, craning their necks with a set of old binoculars while trying to shorten the distance between themselves and their offspring as their child walks across the stage in a procession of graduates.

After the graduation ceremony is over, they reflect on how fast the years of blood, sweat and tears went by, give a long sigh and wish they had the stamina to relive it all over again.

Parents didn't invent the word *enigma* . . . but they don't need a dictionary to understand it.

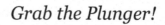

Grab the Plunger!

When I signed up for the school of parenting, I had no idea how extensive the curriculum might become, even though instruction is provided free of charge, and often when you're not exactly paying attention. Here are a few samples from amateurs, like me:

- Teaching children how to *'flush'* is good, but when a child finds joy in watching little *Fisher Price* figures circling the toilet bowl before disappearing, grab the plunger and run at top speed whenever you hear a flush!
- After painting a room, never leave leftover paint cans and a couple of brushes in the hall while you're catching a quick nap. You may awaken to your child putting the finishing touches of paint on prized furniture.
- It's time for a discussion with the driver's ed teacher when your teenager, the one with the brand new driver's permit, comes home from her first lesson behind the wheel exclaiming, *'I'm alive! I'm alive!'*
- Even the top cupboard isn't a safe place to hide matches from the child who wants to burn yarn tassels off the quilt his grandmother made — in order to make his quilt 'a little smoother.'
- Daddy's golf balls and clubs are not designed for backyard play, especially if the neighbors have picture windows.
- Never grab a rubber lizard out of the dryer thinking that it is, actually, rubber.

- On a wet Christmas morning, when several neighbors discover their yards are covered with myriads of little plastic wrappers filled with pink puddles, avoid mentioning to them that your teenage son and his friends bought a case of baby candy canes yesterday and, without checking the weather forecast, went about spreading Christmas cheer on Christmas Eve by hanging tiny candy canes on all the trees in the neighborhood.

For the record, if you don't recognize any of the above lessons in your own curriculum, it's because the repertoire of *'classes'* appears to be tailored to each individual household. That's what keeps parents and their educators in business!

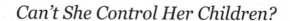

Can't She Control Her Children?

I've been thinking about a question raised in a grocery store checkout line. While observing the behavior of a mother and her unruly children, a fellow shopper turned to me and asked, *'Can't she control her children?'*

Good question, not one to be solved in the express line.

The question first wriggled its way to the top with Adam and Eve in the Garden of Eden, seized a firm hold with Cain and Abel, and continues to demand attention through the tangled thread of centuries.

Shouldn't parents who *'have their children's best interests in mind'* be able to control them? I've tried making peace with this puzzle for . . . let me count the decades.

Parents do their best to provide their children with food, clothing, shelter, safety, health, and education. Along the way, parents model skills, patterns, rules, examples and love so their children can learn how to understand and manage their own thoughts, words and actions. Parents attempt to infuse their children with character, faith, and opportunities for personal development because, after all, their children deserve the best!

As parents, our children belong **with** us, hopefully **learning from** us, but do they belong **to** us? After all, we don't purchase them as if they are horses to *'break'* for our own purposes. They are **not** our property!

It's like this: God has power to control His children, but He doesn't. Maybe that's why we're called human **beings**. God provides clearly stated commandments and then allows us *to be* what we choose to **be.**

Can parents control their children? The *'short game,'* while children are young and need to *'learn the ropes,'* is *'yes'* in any number of circumstances. But the *'long-game'* answer is **no**. They cannot.

Ultimately, human beings can, will, and must choose their own path. It's the plan.

Same Mom and Dad . . . Different Parents

January is a month to ponder beginnings and endings. Our oldest and youngest children, Dan and Janette, were born in January. They have one sister and five brothers sandwiched in between. They have the same mom and dad but were raised by different parents. This is how it went:

When Dan was eight months old, we were concerned. He wasn't crawling yet. In an effort to motivate his development, we lined up paths of miniature marshmallows on the rug and helped him learn how to retrieve them without assistance.

When Janette was eight months old, one of her brothers announced, 'Look, Mom and Dad, Janette can crawl!' We were amazed! How could she possibly be crawling so soon?

Dan took naps as a preschooler. He and I climbed onto his bed with his favorite stack of books, and I read the books until he fell asleep. It usually took about five books. Then, I got up and went back to my important work. Janette took naps, also. We climbed onto my bed with one book, and she turned the pages until I fell asleep. It took a couple of pages, after which she got up and went back to her important work.

At age fifteen, Dan got his driver's license. We were thrilled! He could finally take over many of the carpool duties and errands that met our family's transportation needs.

At age fifteen, Janette wanted to get her driver's license. We held her off as long as we possibly could and complained about silly legislators who pass laws allowing teenagers to drive at such a young age.

Here's what it comes down to in the semi-final analysis.

Parenting techniques come and go like ants at a picnic. What matters most is the glue of love and patience that keeps a family learning together.

Philosophy of Parenting

A friend suggested I write a philosophy of parenting. It turns out that having a written philosophy comes in handy on days I get confused.

After all, it's easier to review details that are written down than to depend upon the details that swirl around in my brain like those *'old maid'* kernels in the bottom of the popper before I pull the plug. Here's my philosophy, the one I keep tweaking:

- Providing children with necessities and comforts is important, but first, teach them to pray.
- The most influential examples come from home.
- Child psychologists write parenting books, but God's scriptures are from the heart of our divine parent who knows everything and every one.
- Little children who learn from little mistakes are less likely to become big children who must learn from big mistakes. (This part came from my wise older brother, Garf.)
- Parents do hard work when their children are small and heart work when their children are grown.
- A good education is important, but trust God for the best learning.
- Children belong **with** their parents but not **to** their parents.
- Your children will never know or remember all you did or do for them, but they will always remember how they felt in your presence.

SECTION 10
PATRIOTIC

This is My Country

This is my country . . .
Where women wear blue jeans or neon bikinis depending on their mood;
Where citizens with disabilities get the best parking spaces;
Where children who can't pay get free lunch at school.

This is my country . . .
Where hatred for people who think and act differently than I do is self-defeating;
Where a flag and goofy bumper stickers are attached to the same car;
Where citizens can dream and plan and work to achieve 'the American dream.'

This is my country . . .
Where wives insist that their husbands take the garbage out . . . now;
Where Christians, Jews, Muslims and atheists eat pizza at the same table;
Where complaining out loud about the government is always in style.

This is my country . . .
Where the only activity shared by the majority is trying to lose weight;
Where leaders are elected by those they serve;
Where pursuing 'life, liberty and the pursuit of happiness' is the standard.

Patriotic

This is my country . . .
Where God has no favorites;
Where prayers are as different as the languages they are spoken in;
Where freedom is holy, and war never will be.

Who Can Fix America?

Was there a time America didn't need to be *'fixed?'* Good question.

When would that time be in the past 250+ years?

After the first American patriots won their battles with Britain?

When *The Constitution* was published?

Before Abraham Lincoln and the Civil War?

During WWI or WWII?

When Martin Luther King's *'I Have a Dream'* speech was given?

After 9/11?

The truth is there probably hasn't been a time in US history when our country didn't *'need to be fixed.'* For evidence, turn on any news station at any time. The newscasters will fill us in on a new list of today's *'things that are broken and need to be fixed right now'* issues. Right after the commercial.

The doctrine of large masses of people governing themselves successfully in a *'liberty and justice for all'* format is relatively new to the world.

'Fixing America' with dollars and cents plus talk and more talk works like rubbing red food coloring onto a yellow apple so that our attention is drawn to the peel of the problems rather than to their core.

Who can fix America?

Not presidents, members of Congress, the CIA, FBI or the Supreme Court.

Not doctors, social workers, teachers, policemen or lawyers.

Not the military, scientists, computer gurus or news media reporters.

Not singers, dancers or actors.

Not even pastors, popes or bishops can fix America.

The core of America is its families. Shortcuts don't work and never will.

Parents, brothers and sisters, aunts and uncles, grandparents, children and grandchildren can steadily work on fixing America, as they have in the past. *'Fixing America'* has to start at home, because democratic systems succeed from the inside out, not from the outside in. They revolve around a core of action where the seeds of positive change and growth are embedded. Every family member plays a part, and every family matters.

America is, was, and ever will be as strong as its individual and collective families. Every family matters. If we lose the strength of the family unit, we will lose the strength of America. That's my opinion, and I'm sticking to it.

As Barbara Bush put it in her famous statement:

"The important thing is not what happens in the White House, but what happens at your house."

Parents Securing the Homeland

My parents should have weaned me out of the *'Mama's* and *Daddy's girl'* stage decades ago, but they keep encouraging it. I'm not complaining.

I was talking to them on the phone last night and started to cry for no reason. Not to be outdone, they started to cry back, because doting parents do that, no matter their ages and stages.

Maybe we were crying because there's so much uncertainty in the big world now, and in my small one, too. There are challenges ahead and hurdles to jump, not to mention pain, loss and adversity. How can ordinary people make sense of this puzzle called life? Is there really such a thing as security?

Similar questions arose when the twin towers of the World Trade Center collapsed into rubble, leaving the innocence of a mighty nation in the dust.

Now, we know the truth. Governments can never keep a promise of security, safety and peace for their citizens absolutely, any more than loving parents can secure carefree lives for their children.

Still, out of the devastation of September 11th rose the courage of millions who are devoted to the principles outlined in *The Declaration of Independence* and *The Constitution*. Americans stand for *'One nation, under God, indivisible, with liberty and justice for all.'* Our faith may quiver, but our resolve to preserve the ideals of freedom has been revisited and revitalized again and again.

One day, I won't be able to access my own twin towers, either. Still, the principles they instilled in me by their examples are like brands to my soul. Education. Integrity. Faith in God. Service. Work. Prayer. Devotion . . . and Love. Yes, I'm a *'Mama's girl'* and a *'Daddy's girl'* and always will be. Even though the outside world may fall short of keeping its promises, striving to follow the example of my parents and the God we worship will provide safety, security and peace . . . and that will be enough.

* Written sometime between 9/11 September 2001 and June, 2004.

A Wanderer's Dream

I close my eyes and picture my homeland,
A wheat field sweeping the corners of the wind,
A mountain sprinkled with a batik of snow,
A ribbon of neon lights competing with the stars.

I see dedicated orchards bearing peaches and pecans,
The plains immersed in a sea of emerald corn,
Velvet meadows speckled by a hundred lazy cows,
The vast expanse of hills and valleys and sagebrush.

I see the pomp and ceremony of color as trees
Stingily relinquish their leaves to cold Mother Earth,
A busy stream perking its cargo with clear purpose
Along its bed toward a distant river.

I close my eyes and picture my homeland,
And with a hollow ache,
I yearn for the moment when I can open them
To the precious landscape of my own America.

* Written in year 3 of our family being stationed overseas with the USAF 1979-81

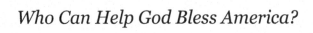

Who Can Help God Bless America?

Who can help God bless America? This task is reserved for people with dedication, patriotism, courage, diligence and love . . . like firefighters, military personnel, policemen, teachers and nurses. But they aren't the only ones who bless the *'land of the free and the home of the brave.'*

My husband and I watched Judy Andrews run a dramatic segment of the Olympic torch relay as it threaded its way toward a cauldron-lighting ceremony in Boise. She had her four young children with her. Their family was stationed at Mountain Home Air Force Base nearby when her husband, Evander Andrews, became the first American casualty in the war against terrorism. Judy has tenacity and patriotism.

Judy helps God bless America.

I met my friend, Bonnie, at a wedding reception, surrounded by her children and grandchildren. They're a happy, congenial clan, and it shows. If I didn't know the facts, I wouldn't believe that both her feet had been amputated less than eighteen months before. Bonnie has courage.

Bonnie helps God bless America.

Every Sunday morning, at 8:58 a.m., my friend, Connie and her husband troop into our chapel on McMillan Road with their four children, all under eight years old. Church starts at 9:00 a.m. Every shoe is tied, every shirt and dress is clean, and every freckle has been polished. Each face sparkles. Connie is diligent.

Connie helps God bless America.

My friend, Carol, wanted a family more than she wanted a promising career as a concert pianist. She is the mother of two and teaches piano to budding musicians. Carol's son, Chris, has cystic fibrosis. His health is fragile and difficult to manage. Carol has learned to appreciate every moment and accept challenges. Carol has love.

Carol helps God bless America.

In every neighborhood across the United States, Americans rise to meet ordinary and extraordinary circumstances with dedication, courage, patriotism, diligence and love.

I believe ordinary American parents help God bless America best.

* Written in the year, 2000.

ABOUT THE AUTHOR

I grew up in the small community of Shelley, Idaho and married my sweetheart, Dan Hawkley, in 1966. We graduated from BYU together in 1969 with degrees in elementary ed. and political science as our parents beamed with pride from the audience while tending our two children.

Later, Dan earned a law degree compliments of the US Air Force and served in the military for 37 years, including twenty years in the Air Force Reserves.

Our eight children were born in Utah, Maine, Nebraska, Michigan, the Philippines, and Idaho. We had the good fortune of raising our children together from birth to maturity. Our 'baby' daughter was married two months before her dad passed away unexpectedly in 2004 at age 60.

I have a Library endorsement certificate from Boise State University, a master's degree in Literacy, and worked as a teacher/librarian at Lowell Scott Middle School from 1998-2011. It was my first 'real job' since our college days.

I enjoy sharing light-hearted messages with those who have an interest in the joys and challenges of parenting. Dan was my cheerleader, suggesting that I 'write something' about whatever we were celebrating or puzzling over in our family, since *'capturing it on paper'* often helps me clarify what is, was or ever-will-be happening on our parenting journey.

The book, <u>*Once Upon an Amateur Mom,*</u> is a collection of writings selected from my *'Mother's Minutes'* newspaper column, magazine articles, letters and email messages published between 1986 and now. I offer them with love and hope to all who are invested in the gift of parenting.

Renee Thomas Hawkley

Note: Most pieces in <u>*Once Upon an Amateur Mom*</u> have been lightly revised from the original publications for ease and clarity.

ACKNOWLEDGEMENTS

Who does an ordinary mom acknowledge when the opportunity to be one is the central experience of her life?

Do I acknowledge my parents, my siblings, my dear husband, Dan Hawkley, and our children, Danny, Jill, Curtis, Clayton, Kyle, Anthony, Ethan and Janette?

Of course! I wouldn't be a mom without them!

Do I acknowledge spouses who married into our family and grandchildren? Yes!

Do I acknowledge my neighbors, schoolmates, teachers, and friends, many of whom are not mothers in the traditional sense, but who *'mother'* plants, animals, birds, bees, other people's children and the earth itself? The list of those people is very long. They know who they are, and I thank each and every all of them!

Mostly, I acknowledge and sincerely appreciate every *'one'* who accepts the gift of being an amateur mom and sees it through as best she can to *The End.*

FULL REVIEWS

'Once Upon an Amateur Mom' is a fabulous tribute to real-life motherhood. Eloquently written, Renee's stories are vivid and entertaining."
—**Blair Wood,** an Investor and a father of two great kids.

"This collection of Renee's experiences as a mom speaks the language of moms everywhere. Family values that teach and inspire are tucked into each page."
—**Carolyn Tanner Reese,** is a mother, grandmother, great-grandmother, BYU graduate, seasoned elementary school teacher and book club member.

"Wonderful! Print it!
—**Charlotte Howard,** Seasoned' English/Lit teacher, mother, grandmother, community service coordinator and always 'up to something good.'

"I laughed, I cried, I agreed and sometimes gave my opinion out loud as I was reading! Once Upon an Amateur Mom *is a delightful collection of everyday-life moments, parenting challenges, family memories, timeless advice, thoughtful words of acceptance, and the power of patriotism, all with a sprinkle of humor."*
—**Cheryl L. Wilson,** is a wife, mother, grandma, volunteer, reader, exercise walker, and friend.

"A family love story . . . past, present and future. Clearly Renee's voice as a mother comes through, but also her voice as a daughter, an American, and a follower of Jesus Christ . . . all presented with thought, humor and not heavy-handed. Her truth is a witness of what has brought her to her knees in both sorrow and gratitude. Her family and faith have brought joy, strength and peace."
—**Delma Atwell,** Mother of six, grandmother of eleven, vegetable and flower gardener, embroidery expert, avid reader, and patriot.

"A delightful read that is real, tender, and cleverly written! I smiled, chuckled, and nodded my head throughout the whole book!"
—**Denise Wyatt,** is a homemaker, a care giver, grandma of ten, and specializes in making quilts.

"What fun tidbits on mothering to bring a smile to my face. I enjoy the wit, the humor, the perspective, and the wisdom Renee shares."
—**Karla Briggs,** is a former elementary ed teacher, a piano teacher, mother of six, and BYU graduate.

"A series of personal family experiences cherished from the past; filled with eternal values that continue today. Hawkley has a way of making a statement the reader can translate into her own experiences."
—**Kathryn L. Eckert**, worked for thirty years as a social worker for the disabled and is the mother of four, grandmother of twelve and great-grandmother of thirteen.

"This is a wonderful compilation of humor, faith and love all brought to us by 'mom.' Heartfelt and honest musings and antidotes on the joy, and sometimes not so joyous occasions of being a mom. I loved every page."
—**Kris Ellis**, is a former Idaho legislator and currently a property manager who loves to read and run in her spare time.

"I thoroughly enjoyed reading this book. What a wonderful, thoughtful and insightful collection of mother musings! It brought back many relatable memories from my own experiences."
—**Monica Brewster,** is a mom, grandma and retired supply chain manager.

"Renee's reflections on motherhood are captivating and refreshing, transcending cultures and generations. With wit and a lively sense of humor, she captures the precious moments when 'young parents' wonder if they are actually 'doing any good' in their early days of parenting."
—**Dr. Vincent Muli Wa Kituku** is a charismatic motivational speaker and author. He shares riveting, inspirational stories from his childhood in Kenya, attaching them to universal messages that touch hearts and change lives for the better. Vincent and his wife brought their family to the United States in search of education and opportunity. While on their way to achieving their own dreams, they yearned to create opportunities for children in Kenya. They were led in faith to establish **Caring Hearts and Hands of Hope**, an organization that promotes and provides education to needy children and teens living in Kenya who would not have the opportunity for education otherwise.
Visit www.caringheartsandhandsofhope.org